Steve Nash

By Jeff Savage

AMAZING ATHLETES

Lerner Publications Company • Minneapolis

Lerner Publications Company
A division of Lerner Publishing Group, Inc.
241 First Avenue North
Minneapolis, MN 55401 U.S.A.

Website address: www.lernerbooks.com

Library of Congress Cataloging-in-Publication Data

Savage, Jeff, 1961–
    Steve Nash / by Jeff Savage.
        p.   cm. — (Amazing athletes)
    Includes index.
    ISBN-13: 978–0–8225–5956–6 (lib. bdg. : alk. paper)
    ISBN-10: 0–8225–5956–0 (lib. bdg. : alk. paper)
    1. Nash, Steve, 1974– —Juvenile literature. 2. Basketball players—United States—Biography—Juvenile literature. I. Title. II. Series.
    GV884.N37 2007
    796.323'092—dc22   2005037281

Manufactured in the United States of America
 3 4 5 6 7 – DP – 12 11 10 09 08 07

TABLE OF CONTENTS

Steve looks for an opening against Dallas Mavericks guard Jason Terry in Game 6.

A Hot Sun

Steve Nash raced up the court dribbling the basketball. His mop of hair flopped around his head. In a blink, he fired a pass to teammate Shawn Marion. Marion tossed the ball in for an easy **layup**. Seconds later, Steve steamed up the court again. The Phoenix Suns **point guard** stopped at the **three-point line**. He rose up with the ball and let it fly. Swish! The Phoenix Suns took a 106–105 lead. There was one minute left in the game.

The crowd at American Airlines Arena in Dallas, Texas, was in shock. Just minutes ago, Steve's team, the Suns, had trailed the Dallas Mavericks by 16 points. It looked like the Mavericks would win Game 6 of this 2005 **playoff** series.

But with Steve's magical dribbling and unselfish play, the high-flying Suns had come all the way back. The Mavericks scored four quick points to take a 109–106 lead with 27 seconds left. The Suns needed to score. Steve drove headlong toward the hoop.

He spun in a layup. Dallas's lead was down to one. Mavericks guard Jerry Stackhouse sank two **free throws** to put Dallas back up by three. Nine seconds were left in the game. The clock was ticking.

Steve takes the ball to the hoop for a layup in Game 6.

Steve works for a shot against the Mavericks' Jason Terry.

Steve sprinted up the court with the ball. Dallas players surrounded him. Steve pulled up and shot a three-pointer. It was good! The game was tied, 109–109! The game went into **overtime**. The teams would play five more minutes. Dallas fans feared the worst. They knew what Steve could do. He had spent six years playing for the Mavericks. But in this game, he was creating new excitement with the Suns.

Steve took control in overtime. First, he nailed another three-pointer. Next, he got the Mavericks players to move toward him. This left Steve's teammate Shawn Marion open for a three-point shot. Steve flipped the pass to Shawn, who made the shot. Then Steve drilled a running jump shot. With just a few seconds left, Mavericks forward Dirk Nowitzki missed a shot. Steve snatched the **rebound** and was **fouled**. He sank both free throws. The Suns won, 130–126.

It was a close and stressful game. But Steve loved every minute of it. "I have had so much fun with my new teammates this year," Steve said. "I just love being a part of a team, any team."

Steve and his brother, Martin *(above)*, grew up playing soccer. Martin plays soccer for the Vancouver Whitecaps.

LEARNING TO DRIBBLE

Steven John Nash grew up dribbling—with his feet. He was born February 7, 1974, in Johannesburg, South Africa. His childhood was all about soccer. His father, John, played professional soccer. His brother, Martin, plays professionally. According to Steve's mother, Jean, the first word Steve said was "Goal!"

Steve grew up in Victoria, British Columbia. One of its most famous landmarks is the Sunken Garden *(above)* at Butchart Gardens.

When Steve was one year old, his family moved to Canada. They lived in Victoria, British Columbia. Victoria is on the southwestern tip of Canada, along the Pacific Ocean. It is about 20 miles from the United States.

Basketball is not a hugely popular game in Canada. Steve spent much of his childhood playing many sports, including hockey, baseball, lacrosse, and rugby. He seemed to be great at any sport he played. He was voted most valuable player of his junior high soccer team. He even won three chess titles!

Steve wanted to become great at something. "I was inspired by reading other people's stories," he said. "I liked how they worked hard, how they overcame obstacles."

Steve enjoyed basketball above all. By his senior year at St. Michaels University High School, he had become a star point guard. He averaged 21 points, 11 **assists**, and nine rebounds. He led his team to the British Columbia championships.

Steve *(front, second from left)* and his teammates celebrate after winning the British Columbia championships.

Steve was clearly good enough to play for a college team. But few Canadian colleges had top-level teams. His high school coach, Ian Hyde-Lay, knew Steve was good enough to play for an American school. Hyde-Lay made phone calls and sent letters to many colleges. He asked them to **recruit** Steve. But no one did. Steve was frustrated.

One college coach finally showed up to watch Steve play. It was Dick Davey from Santa Clara University in northern California. Coach Davey was impressed with Steve's speed and ballhandling skills and offered him a **scholarship**. Steve was grateful.

Steve fights off Maryland's
Laron Profit *(left)*.

LITTLE MAGIC

Santa Clara's players weren't as big, strong,
and talented as players from the powerhouse
schools like UCLA, Stanford, and Arizona.
Steve and his teammates had to win by
outhustling and outthinking their opponents.

During Steve's **freshman** year, Santa Clara surprised everyone by reaching the 1993 **NCAA Men's Basketball Tournament**. In the first game, Santa Clara shocked the mighty Arizona Wildcats. Steve sealed the victory by making six straight free throws in the final 31 seconds.

As a **sophomore**, Steve worked hard to improve his skills. He even dribbled a tennis ball from class to class. He was enjoying college life. "I have a lot of interests—in books, music, current

Steve dribbles past another player during the NCAA Men's Basketball Tournament.

Steve drives the ball around Maryland's Terrell Stokes.

events," he said. "I find things fascinating. I like to learn." When Steve was not studying, he was in the gym late at night. He shot hundreds of baskets. The hard work paid off. In one game as a **junior**, Steve made 21 straight free throws. In another, he drilled 8 three-pointers and scored 40 points. With his fancy ballhandling, he led the Santa Clara Broncos to the NCAA tournament again.

Steve's exciting style of play was getting him noticed. The Broncos opened the 1995–1996 season at the Maui Invitational Tournament in Hawaii. The day before the first game, Steve met former NBA superstar Magic Johnson. Steve got his picture taken with Johnson. Later, Johnson signed the photo: "Good luck from Big Magic to Little Magic."

That season, the Broncos were ranked as one of the **Top 25** teams for the first time in 23 years. Steve capped his amazing college career by setting the school's career record for assists.

Magic Johnson *(left)* was a point guard for the Los Angeles Lakers. He gave Steve the nickname Little Magic.

Steve was drafted in 1996 by the Phoenix Suns.

REACHING HIS DREAM

While in college, Steve often thought of playing in the pros. "The NBA is the major dream in my life," he said. With the 15th pick in the 1996 NBA **Draft**, the Phoenix Suns chose Steve.

Steve says basketball is "all about having fun. Having fun is competing, having fun is challenging yourself, having fun is being a good teammate."

Playing in the NBA was not much fun for Steve at first. He mostly sat on the bench. The Suns' two star point guards, Kevin Johnson and Jason Kidd, played ahead of him. Steve started in just one game his first season. He made the most of this chance, scoring 17 points and grabbing 12 rebounds. But he mostly sat on the bench.

His second year was nearly the same. He did display a great shooting touch, especially from the free throw line. He led the team by making nearly 9 of every 10 of his foul shots. But Johnson and Kidd were great players too. The Suns just didn't have much playing time for Steve.

Meanwhile, other teams had noticed Steve's skills. Before the 1998–1999 season, the Suns traded Steve to the Dallas Mavericks. The Mavericks were struggling. They hadn't had a winning season in nearly 10 years. They believed Steve could lift them to the playoffs. They signed him to a six-year contract for $33 million. Steve was rich beyond his wildest dreams. But he was more excited about getting a chance to play.

Steve scores two points for his new team, the Dallas Mavericks.

Steve's first two years in Dallas were a struggle. He suffered from a painful foot injury.

By the end of his second season in Dallas, Steve began to feel better. It was just in time to play for the Canadian team in the 2000 **Olympic Games** in Sydney, Australia. Steve led Team Canada to upset victories over Yugoslavia, Russia, Australia, and Spain. Steve's team finally lost when the French team **triple-teamed** him.

Steve returned from the Olympics with longer hair and a new attitude. His success had made him more confident.

Steve celebrates after Canada's win over Yugoslavia.

Steve *(left)* talks with Mavericks' star Dirk Nowitzki.

In the 2000–2001 season, he doubled his scoring. Steve scored nearly 16 points per game. He still delivered passes every way possible—underhanded, behind his back, even bouncing the ball through opponents' legs. Steve and sharpshooters Dirk Nowitzki and Michael Finley became known as the Mavericks' Big Three. In 2001, they reached the playoffs for the first time in years.

The Mavericks became a top NBA team. Steve's moves made his team fun to watch. After the 2003–2004 season, Steve became a free agent. He could join any other team that wanted him. The Phoenix Suns offered him a six-year contract for $60 million. Steve signed the deal. "I didn't want to leave Dallas," Steve said. "But joining the Suns was best for me."

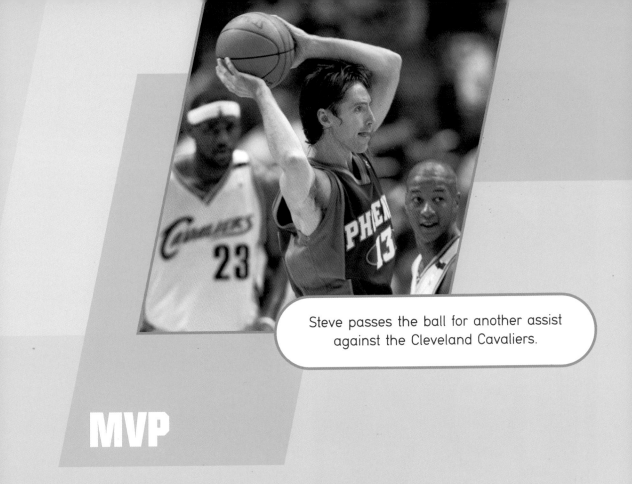

Steve passes the ball for another assist against the Cleveland Cavaliers.

MVP

The Suns were a lousy team. They had a record of 29–53 in 2003–2004. Steve changed everything. He led the NBA with more than 11 assists per game. This was the most assists per game in 10 years. With Steve running the show, the Suns collected a league-best 62 wins. The team had made an amazing turnaround.

During the 2005 playoffs, the winner of the NBA Most Valuable Player Award was announced. Steve topped Shaquille O'Neal and others to win the award. Steve was given his trophy before one of the Suns' games. He called his teammates onto the court to receive the award with him. "This is really a reflection of this group," Steve announced to the crowd. "Thanks, fellows!"

The Suns lost to the San Antonio Spurs in the 2005 Western Conference Finals. But Steve earned their respect. "You have to be ready when you play against Steve Nash," said Spurs guard Tony Parker, "because you're going to do a lot of chasing."

Steve goes up against the Spurs' Tony Parker *(left)* during the 2005 Western Conference Finals.

Steve didn't let up for the 2005–2006 season. He led the NBA in assists. His skills and leadership helped the Suns win 54 games.

The Suns went into the playoffs. After beating  the Lakers in a tough seven-game series, Steve received some exciting news. He had been voted the NBA's Most Valuable Player again! Only eight other players have won the award two years in a row. "Steve is not just a great player," said Suns chairman Jerry Colangelo. "He's one of

Steve makes a difficult pass around Kris Humphries *(left)* of the Utah Jazz.

Steve puts on a suit and tie for a Men of the Year celebration in 2005.

the few players . . . who makes everyone better around him."

Steve also works to make the world a better place. He created the Steve Nash Foundation to help kids. The organization provides money for projects that make life better for lots of kids. The projects include helping to build a place for kids to play basketball in Toronto, Canada. The foundation also paid for improvements to a hospital in his wife Alejandra's home country of Paraguay.

Steve eats healthy food to stay strong and fast. But on special occasions, he treats himself to M&Ms or apple pie with ice cream.

Steve stays fast by running and lifting weights at his home in Scottsdale, Arizona. He lives there with Alejandra and their twin daughters, Lourdes and Isabella. Steve's parents live in a house a few blocks away. There is no secret to Steve's greatness. It is strictly hard work. "A player with determination and a willingness to work harder than anyone else can accomplish anything," Steve says. "Believe in yourself, have a plan, stick to it, and you can accomplish a lot more than you or others expect you to."

Selected Career Highlights

2005–2006
Named NBA Most Valuable Player for second straight season
Named to All-NBA first team
Named to the NBA All-Star team for fourth time
Led league with 10.5 assists per game
Scored a career-high 18.8 points a game

2004–2005
Named NBA Most Valuable Player
Named first-team All-NBA
Named to the NBA All-Star team for third time
Named Western Conference Player of the Month for November
Led league with 11.5 assists per game

2003–2004
Ranked third in the NBA in assists with career-high 8.8 average
Had 19 assists against Sacramento Kings, the most assists in a game that season
Tied Mavericks team record for most three-pointers in a game without a miss (5)

2002–2003
Named to NBA All-Star team for second time

2001–2002
Named to the NBA All-Star team for first time
Averaged career-high 17.9 points per game
Was only Mavericks player to start all 82 games

2000–2001
Averaged career-high 15.6 points per game
Ranked fourth in the NBA in free throw shooting, making nearly 9 out of every 10 free throws

1999–2000
Scored in double figures in 15 of last 20 games of the season

1998–1999
Led the Mavericks in assists with 219

1997–1998
Ranked 13th in NBA in three-point shooting, hitting more than 4 out of 10 three-pointers (a .415 percentage)
Led Suns in free throw shooting, hitting nearly 9 out of 10 free throws (an .860 percentage)

1996–1997
Fifteenth player taken in NBA draft

Glossary

assists: passes to teammates that help score baskets

draft: a yearly event in which professional sports teams take turns choosing new players from a selected group

fouled: hit in a way that is against the rules. A player who is fouled usually gets to shoot free throws.

free throws: shots taken from behind the free throw line

freshman: first-year student

junior: third-year student

layup: a shot made by placing the ball into the hoop or bouncing the ball off the backboard

NCAA Men's Basketball Tournament: end-of-the-season competition in which 65 teams play to decide the national champion of college basketball

Olympic Games: an event held every four years in which athletes from around the world compete in dozens of different sports

overtime: extra time played to decide the winner of a game

playoff: a postseason tournament held to decide the NBA championship. The NBA playoff system has four rounds, and a team must win four games in each round to win the championship.

point guard: the player on a basketball team who is responsible for running the team's scoring plays. Point guards are skilled at dribbling and passing the ball.

rebound: grabbing a missed shot

recruit: to invite a high school student to play a sport at a college

scholarship: an award that helps pay for a student's college fees

sophomore: second-year student

three-point line: a line on the court that marks the three-point basket range. Any shot made from behind the three-point line earns three points.

Top 25: the best 25 college teams in the country, as voted by coaches and sportswriters

triple-teamed: guarded by three players

Further Reading & Websites

Berry, Skip. *Kids' Book of Basketball: Skills, Strategies, Equipment, and the Rules of the Game.* New York: Citadel Press, 2001.

Hareas, John. *Basketball.* New York: DK Publishing, 2005.

NBA Website
http://www.nba.com
The NBA's website provides fans with recent news stories, statistics, biographies of players and coaches, and information about games.

Sports Illustrated for Kids
http://www.sikids.com
The *Sports Illustrated for Kids* website covers all sports, including basketball.

Steve Nash Charity Organization
http://www.stevenash.org
This website shows how Steve helps children in need.

Index

Photo Acknowledgments

Photographs are used with the permission of: © Jeff Mitchell/Reuters/CORBIS, p. 4; © Brad Loper/*The Dallas Morning News*, p. 6; © David Guzman/*The Dallas Morning News*, p. 7; © Rik Fedyck/WireImage.com, p. 9; © Todd Gipstein/National Geographic/Getty Images, p. 10; St. Michaels University School Archives, p. 11; © Craig Hacker/TSN/Icon SMI, pp. 13, 14, 15; © Neal Preston/CORBIS, p. 16; AP/Wide World Photos, p. 17; © Reuters/CORBIS, pp. 19, 20; © Hector Amezcua/*The Sacramento Bee*/ZUMA Press, p. 21; © Jay Drowns/*The Sporting News*/ZUMA Press, p. 23; © Jeff Topping/Reuters/CORBIS, p. 24; © William Luther/*San Antonio Express*/ZUMA Press, p. 25; © George Frey/epa/CORBIS, p. 26; © Steve Granitz/WireImage.com, p. 27; © Chris Hatfield/Icon SMI/CORBIS, p. 29.

Front Cover: © Chris Hatfield/Icon SMI.